BeautySong

A Collection of Lyrical Poetry

by

Skot David Wilson

BeautySong

Published by Skot David Wilson
ISBN: 978-1-304-88882-2
Title: BeautySong
Author: Skot David Wilson
Publisher: Skot David Wilson through Lulu

Other Titles by Skot David Wilson

(as eBooks)
Fiction & Fantasy:
Before Atlantis
Exit Strategy
2180, A Future Reborn
Memoirs:
1978, Crossing America and Back
1985, An Atlantic Crossing
Walls Go Up, Walls Come Down
Poetry:
BeautySong
Dust

(as imprints)
BeautySong in 6" by 9" or 8.5" by 11"
Utopian Trilogy: Before Atlantis; Exit Strategy;
and, 2180, A Future Reborn

(available at LuLu.com among other places)
eBooks available at smashwords.com, Barnes & Noble, and many other sources

Foreword & Author Statement

I was raised in a small town by the name of Union Beach, New Jersey, w directly South by water from New York City across the Raritan Bay. I was born early in 1961, which allowed me the unique opportunity to watch the world's transition from analogue to digital. I was fortunate enough to grow up in the Zenith of American civilization and prosperity to date. I was also lucky enough to have loving parents, and the freedom to expand my horizons, and even when my parents disagreed with some of my decisions, the support to make my own decisions. The secret blessing about growing up middle class is that neither poverty nor excessive wealth blinded my perspective. I was also raised with a strong faith in God, but questioned traditional religion and soon became a Unitarian-Universalism. I also consider myself a little bit of a Taoist in spiritual philosophy, and have reclaimed a good deal of my Episcopalian perspectives and traditions. I see what or who we call "God" as universal, and all religions as incomplete. I believe I understand the message of all major world religions, having studied and practiced faith with Muslims, Hindus, Sekhs, Conservative Christians, Jews, and Buddhists.... How so many can say the same thing and still disagree dumbfounds me.

I also grew up reading a series of philosophers and read the entire set by age 12. This set me apart from others. As a young boy I played in the marshes of the Raritan Bay, and every summer our family would travel and spend real time camping in different regions of the country. I was blessed to spend time in the Amish Country of Pennsylvania, in New England, and see cultural and historic sites, places as unique as Hershey, Pennsylvania, The Grand Ole' Oprey, Luray Caverns, Mystic Seaport, Atlantic City, The Smithsonian and many other historical sites in Washington, D.C. And Philadelphia, and Gettysburg and other battlefields, not to mention New York City and the wealth of culture it stores. My imagination and mind's eye allowed me to grasp civilization in context of change over time, and make good estimations of things to come.

In my hometown there was also a chemical factory where an accidental explosion shook my home over a mile away. I remember the rainbow oily sheen of pollution in the water and in the rich, dark, aerobic mud. I remember the wildlife, the bounty of sealife, with clarity. My father worked in a lead paint pigment factory, and he died, like many of his co-workers, before reaching 60 at 57 when I was 17. This event made me resentful and angry and anarchistic. The bitterness I felt almost destroyed me. Before his death, I put my ideals into practice, and was suspended from school for refusing to remove my hat as long as female students weren't required to do the same. The ERA was a big issue at the time, and I felt the issue was reverse gender based double standards. I promoted a concert to benefit World Hunger Year starring Harry Chapin just before my 16th. Birthday, and was chosen to represent my school as a Hugh O'Brian Youth Leader at a leadership seminar for students with the most leadership potential, and while there earned a reputation for being outspoken and well informed on a wide range of topics. I was a member of Clearwater, Amnesty International, and fought for social justice, protection of the environment, against world hunger, and for conflict resolution.

I had dropped out of the 11th grade, took my GED in order to attend college early. My father died in June of 1978. I left home and traveled,. When I returned home I started college, getting involved in a civics in the town I was living in, protesting the re-introduction of selective service registration among other things, but I was young and was not well focused. Still angry over the death of my father and doing way too many recreational drugs, made serious mistakes and lost a great relationship. I had ideals for the most part lived by and lost my way. After suffering from my mistakes found my way. I think I've been making good progress ever since.

I follow my conscience and try to live with it clear. I have traveled, studied, faced and witnessed death and some of the worst of humanity, but have seen bravery, honor, dignity, compassion, and those things which make us great. This collection draws from experiences and are based on my belief in Love as the greatest of all human emotions, a belief that without Equity, Integrity, Compassion, and Humility that Love can not long endure or flourish, and that without it we are beasts, and not worthy of the blessings this life allows us. I hope to inspire others as I have been inspired, and hope I remind people of the qualities within themselves which gave me the passion to write these down in the first place.

For my father, Alfred Duncan Wilson 1921-1978

Who before he died, knowing he was dying, left me with a lesson of wisdom,
in which he said,
"Your most valuable possession is your name:
You can't buy a good one, and you can't sell a bad one"

For my mother, Gloria Chandler, formerly Wilson, nee' LaGiglia

She gave me the love and freedom to grow into who I have become.

To my grandmother, Florence (Nana) Wilson, nee' McFarland 1901-1984

She always had faith in me, and gave me hope in some of my darkest days.

Dedicated to my son, Alexander Orion Wilson

May he find peace and acceptance, a balance between pride and humility, true purpose, and the courage to shape his world into one of joy and accomplishment.

Contents

"BeautySong"

**I thought I'd sing, a BeautySong,
in the pastel fires of autumn's sunset,
to quell the flames of my regrets.**

**But regrets are merely wishes gone wrong,
to such an endeavor, I shan't belong.
So the thought progressed, to what could be,
if I gave to others, the good inside me.**

**I began to sing, a BeautySong.....
With vibrant voice,
harmony abounds by choice,
these words to which we must belong....
Freedom,
Peace,
Compassion,
Love........**

This is, The BeautySong

"Dignity and Worth"

I believe in the dignity, and believe in the worth,
of every human spirit, drawing breath on earth.

I believe in truth and justice, freedom and equity,
supersedes greed or hate, jealousy or bigotry.

I believe we have free will, and our inherent right.
to live as we choose to live, and to seek in the darkness---light;

and when we infringe upon the rights of others, that our right to freedom ends,
to the oppressed we have a duty to stand with courage and defend.

I believe every scripture, every teaching, every creed in every land,
shares basics values and can teach lessons to every woman, every man.

Ultimately it is we ourselves who choose what path we take,
and by our conscience and our deeds hell or heaven make.

That it does not matter what religion, race, preference, or gender, any may choose to be;
that we are one blood, one earth, one people,
root to branch---one tree.

“Looking For God”

Everybody goes looking for God....
Each has their own way, each has their own say,
'bout what they believe....

Everybody has the right to their own voice,
the right to their own choice,
and the only absolute is what we call "mystery"

If every little secret were known,
the faith would be pointless, love couldn't be shown,
and no hopes be carried out, life's tests remove the doubt,
'bout who's kind, or not,
You can find a lot,
when conscience comes,
and you suffer not in vain,
cause out of the pain, you can find......
one heart,
one reason,
and one mind.....

Everybody goes looking for the truth,
as only life can show it,
life let's you know it,
as only it can,
when you open up your heart,
dear friend

"Midnight Fire"

Red and amber the radiant warmth
of this midnight fire,
with wisps of white, blue, yellow, and green,
glowing with snaps and pops,
as the chemical reaction of oxidation
returns carbon from the source of it's capture.......

We gather around the fire as if drawn by primal instincts,
at ease with each other,
or at peace with our own solitude....
Time seems to slow,
and a mix of both numbness and clarity form,
in the orbital glow......

Smoke and embers skyward rise,
like prayers ascend to Heaven,
silently carrying pleading or praise,
contingent upon mood and emotions......
I am alert and my mind races,
without any commotion.

I am insulated from the trappings I have made for myself,
as if somehow reconnected,
with the fire within my own soul.

"StoryBook Affair"

Why can't love be a storybook affair,
the prince and the princess, magic in the air.
Why can't two hearts beat as one,
each day a new beginning, each day love songs sung.

Yet there's this world in the back of my mind,
and the front of my dreams,
where each day I find, and it always seems,
that when I wake up alone, to face another day,
this house ain't no home....
I need a new place to stay,
I need a new place to stay.

Why can't love be a storybook affair,
the love and the lovers, magic everywhere
like from some black and white movie, in a time of long ago,
where two souls touch truly, and Love's true beauty flows.......

Yet there's this world in the back of my mind,
and the front of my dreams,
where each day I find, that it always seems,
that when I wake up alone, to face another day,
this house ain't no home.....
I need a new place to stay,
I need a new place to stay

"It Feels Good"

There's misinterpretations floating through my head,
this thought, that,
am I alive or dead...
Social restrictions try to put my mind to bed.
Stop and go and yes and no,
and what was really said.

Who can tell me, who can know,
where the truth lies at, and what I am to show?
Teach to me and preach to me,
your words are all the same,
you inflict me with your standards,
it's just a silly game.

Hell, no................no, no more.
I won't stay weak, and I won't stay on the floor,
hey, yo,   I'm out the door,
I just can't take it,   no, no more.
To have a mind, then you choose to use it,
to have a power, with a faith that won't abuse it,
to hear good news,
that's coming through,
with the power to lead you on-a,
back to you

To find your own soul, and the mind to refine it,
to wind up whole, and a spirit to define it,
to live life good, just like you should,
be all you could, clear conscience true.

It feels good, finding a second choice,
It feels good, I'm speaking in my own voice
It feels good, I'm getting away from the pain,
It feels good being me again

It feels good, I'm getting away from the past,
It feels good being me at last,
I see it all, with message clear coming through,
I'm standing strong, with a heart that is true,
I know my path, and the things in life I must do,
and it feels good...........

"Star of Love"

I sing to myself, lovesongs in the dark,
the night so alone,
it's always coldest before the dawn....
The sun appears over the horizon like a spark,
lights the day, I'm on the way to the heart.

Visions you, in promises of two,
here in my silent heart,
(lies) this love of me and you,
so find now this heart,
lying broken in parts,
when ever I wake alone,
first vulnerable, then prone, to,
shivers from the cold winds of being so far,
from the warmth of the Love Star
As I wait for seasons change,
gentle spring rains,
come lead me back to you,
let your love flow, and shine,
like the Star of Love shines, so shine,
sweet radiant Star of Love, shine,
shine on me

There's a calling to answer, through reaches of space,
beheld by such beauty, bring tears to my face,
love lit from heaven, starlit from above,
come turn my world into a paradise of love that shines,
like the Star of Love shines,
shine, sweet radiant Star of Love, shine, shine on me

And my dreams of you, they hold me through,
as the darkest times are with out you,
as I wait for seasons change,
those gentle spring rains
as I wait for you to come, so I can be done,
then to bask in the rays of the sweet Love Sun,
that shines, like the Start of Love, just shines,
so shine, sweet radiant Star of Love, shine,
shine on me,
shine on me, shine on me,
shine on me

"In My Life's Story"

I have been a witness to the fury of the storm
and I have been relentless as the coming of the dawn
and I have seen the sunshine break through dark clouds above
and I have known the shades between hatred and true love
and through all these chapters that I've written in the book of my life's story
I've seldom fully understood….
the thin line between bad and good….
and the perspective that defines, shame and glory…..

I have sought to understand what makes a man a man….
and I have been undone by conscience comes, when it gets hard to stand
and I have heard the arguments between emotion, fear, and truth…
and I have made my choices when commotion clearly ruled
and I have stood below above and sometimes above below
and through all the pages that I've turned this is what I've come to know
the thin line between bad and good….. can be so easily understood…..
it's perspective that defines, what is shame and what is glory….
in my life's story
In my life's story……. **oh, the races I have run**
In my life's story……. **I have lost and I have won**
In my life's story……. **If I could stand then I risk to fall**
In my life's story……. **savored the wonder of it all**
In my life's story……. **I have laughed and I have cried**
In my life's story…… **and I will live until I die**
In my life's story…….
I have been a wild child with way too much to say
and now I have a quiet smile, as I turn old, bald and gray……
and I have seen how wisdom comes if allowed to grow
and I have been somehow satisfied with these things I've come to know
and I have found this simple truth, you get more when you give
and those who take in selfishness do not know how to live
we each have a pen and have a page and a legacy to leave
and what we write as our own story,
each choice we make…. each act we take….
depends on what we each believe
In my life's story……. **oh, the races I have run**
In my life's story……. **I have lost and I have won**
In my life's story……. **If I could stand then I risk to fall**
In my life's story……. **savored the wonder of it all**
In my life's story……. **have laughed and I have cried**
In my life's story……. **and I will live until I die**
In my life's story……

"Middle of the Atlantic"

Two miles of water under the hull,
and 2,000 miles of blue water away from either North America or Europe...
Being so isolated I never felt so much a part of the Earth.
2,000 miles into a 15,000 plus mile journey,
A 28 foot Shannon Cutter my only island.
I wanted away, and a friend wanted help sailing, so I left without a word.
Things that had happened, how could I tell anyone?
I had too much to deal with or share, so I left in secret.
I just needed to go.
In the middle of the Atlantic I stared into the oceanic abyss,
and found peace.

On my sojourn I encountered different cultures.
I saw what was the same, and what was distinct and unique.
I saw vast wealth and extreme poverty.
I saw the ravages of war, and the blessings of peace.

I have made love to women on four continents,
and danced on four continents.
I have felt my smallness, and my immensity.
I have felt the eternal constants,
and lived by the clock of the sky and sea.

Tossed about like a piece of cork on a raging sea, hard rains and wind,
knowing if the small cutter sank no one would know and I would be lost forever,
and my body would return to the earth and sea from which it came.
In the calm after a storm I gave myself to the light and endless stars,
I felt connected to the Universe.
There was solitude and absolute calm with no wind it the doldrums,
and I knew I could not explain or share this with anyone, at least back then.

Naked on desolate beaches,
I as vulnerable as the first man, and as powerful.

How can I explain what I found to anyone? I can only say 'I did this thing".
My secret sojourn, to discover who I was.
I had to let go of myself to find what I was looking for.
I found the ability to forgive others, and myself,
In the middle of the Atlantic.

“Shark River Island”

**I was away from the Jersey Shore for too long,
and the waters that defined me.
Returning from Williamsburg, I looked again to the sea,
and found where I needed to be, on Shark River Island.**

**Lobstering with Wacker,
building bulkheads and the occasional charter run,
Kayaking to the beach at Belmar, dancing at night,
a rouge environmental activist,
making use of skills I learned in another life,
attacking the powerful as a warrior,
and suffering consequences of standing against the storm,
suffering both injustice and my own stupidity.**

**There I was, a 1967 24 foot Trojan, twin 318 Crusaders, and on the water.
A life of freedom and adventure, a dream, yet something was missing.**

**I placed a distance between myself and my family and friends,
I chose to be alone when I didn't have to be.
A desire to find closeness married to a fear of the same,
I would not accept compromise, and that was my wall.
So I left, moved 1,000 miles away, because I knew I needed more.**

**Maybe I had seen too much, experienced too much,
or maybe I just didn't know how to share it, or myself.
Over a quarter of a century and I still feel a level of separation.
Maybe I just love my solitude,
and simply need someone who can understand how to share it with me.**

**Away from the water I am adrift, and long for the sea.
Love is my one true compass, but there are magnetic deviations,
and I don't have a chart.
So I sail by dead reckoning,
seeking that safe harbor, that friendly port, where I can anchor.**

**A new boat, chart my course, and set sail for new shores....
and finish the building ship I started to build,
on Shark River Island.**

“My Union Beach Christmas…….”

**Nativity on the mantle, sitting upon cotton “supposed-to-be” snow,
figurines in an surreal life, waiting for Santa in stillness-soft lights, glow
revealing idyllic visions of Yule….. time seems to slow I am a child then,
in this memory, and again, and again… and again………
every time Thanksgiving passes….
especially after the last cold turkey on toast is eaten
and when I hear the first Christmas song on the radio or in a store’s
muzak….
my mother taping Christmas cards to the inside of the front door
hanging lights with my father,
Nana’s Apple Scoop….
Dr. Pepper warm with lemon and orange slices
Yes,
Yes I will have a Very Merry Christmas,
and I’m dreaming of a white one as well…
It is beginning to look a lot like Christmas…
and I think I can tell…
People act a little nicer to each other,
more at ease to say “hello”
Christmas lights, cinnamon and spice, holly and mistletoe…
I remember that aluminum tree,
and the color wheel slowly turning green to blue to yellow to red….
so many memories churning….
Uncle Johnnie going all out with decorations,
and yes,
even real chestnuts
Claymation Rudolph seems just like a friend,
and Charlie Brown and Peanuts….
my father enjoyed his cookies and milk, he earned them, every crumb…
and graffiti on window frost,
until vanished by the sun
and waking up early, the mad rush to the tree,
I am a child then, in this memory,
I am a child again, when this season comes around here,
but halfway back to Union Ave and I can hear the sound……..
Union Beach whispers,
in my ear and then again I am a child inside,
and if you listen, you’ll hear…
The Soul of Christmas confide the Secret of the Season
which shines and glistens like lights and tinsel….
and I will listen, and again and again… and again…….
I am a child then**

" and I remember………"

**I remember….
the tide is out and I'm ready to dig…..
I jump, watching next the geysers on the flat sands.
I run to them and dig with shovel and-or hands….
Piss clams**

**I remember….
Matty's creek and a seine net and killifish and spearing
and my father and I in the dark sulfur egg mud,
as fiddlers danced
hearing gulls, wind, and the breath of my beloved Bayshore**

**I remember….
Sunday morning going to Ralph's for a paper,
steering the Country Squire home on my father's lap,
that left turn, then parking,
before going inside to cut and butter a perfect hardroll,
as a Silly Putty transfer of Dondi or Dick Tracy became distorted
as I pull and pull
before I store it back in the plastic egg….**

**I remember so well that I am there,
walking in a parade in my Twins uniform,
gray and maroon, the itchy wool….
the smell of the marsh….
the fire engines and bands and everyone with little American flags
waving…
Trick or Treat, a pillowcase of sweets,
and the Castle…….**

**It's 8 O'clock, and three siren blasts
and I have about 10 minuets to get home,
and I think everyone else is hauling ass as well…..
Norman Rockwell could not paint such perfection,
with colors of characters so warm**

**The tide came in, like never before,
but my memories can never be washed away……
They stay….   and new ones I never will know are formed,
they are mine, although I have no part in their creation,
because they are formed in shared legacy.
My Borough is my family,**

"Here we are.... Transitions"

Here we are,
where we are,
not where we'd thought we'd be....
Home is where the heart is, they say,
and this now is what we see....

A resident transformed into a neighbor,
a neighbor into a friend,
a friend becoming part of family,
and a family without end......

Here we are,
we've come so far,
from those places good and/or bad....

We gather round this time of year to share stories happy and/or sad...
We find our seat at a table, ready for a seasonal feast...
Remembering words said long ago about what ye do unto the least.....

We seat ourselves in good company, are warmed by the meeting of eyes,
they say so much with wordless exchanges, about that which never dies...
We give thanks as we remember, that possessions come and go
but what defines us is so much more than "things", and to each other show....
Thanks,
for all we have, even nothing,
because when all is lost what remains
is our simple heart, and that's our home,
and a family that sustains.......

A resident transformed into a neighbor,
a neighbor into a friend,
a friend becoming part of family,
and a family without end......

“This Same Water”

**I was looking at the St. John’s River today, wide as it is,
and flashed an epiphany of connection….
If I had a boat I could sail to the Raritan Bay,
where Union Beach lives,
if a possible choice this would be my election.
Mapquest says 950 miles,
but through screen, keys, and mouse
I’m there, so close but yet so far
and my thought of by boat just made me smile,
if life permitted I’d jump in my car……
Another funny thought,
about water and land, surrounded on three sides,
where I once stood and now stand
This same water, joined as we are,
like the view of the moon, breath of air sight of star….
This same water which shapes the outlines of these states,
slowly constant change destroys and creates.
This same water, with a thought I am home,
I can see a face through a voice on the phone…
This same water, yet stronger ties through we bind,
when the worst comes to find us the best do we find…..
This same water against us cannot win,
when it comes to end, we again begin…
I went to see Andrew, homes razed to the ground.
I remember the silence, tears the only sound
I went to Alberto where I saw death,
carried it away, and the next day was at play.
I went down to Tampa,
Depression Number One,
and when twisters hit Jax it wasn’t much fun
I went to the Black Creek, saw what Fay washed away,
and this year came Debby, 25 ft flood stage
I went when I was able and did what I could,
I saw humanity’s wide range from bad to so good…..
and as I looked at the river,
all these thoughts blend, so I know what is lost
and what I must send,
and I watch as so many stand up oh, so proud…
UB tough, Jersey Strong,
the words said so loud....**

(“This Same Water” Continued)

**This same water binds us,
when I see it I know, that our best often finds us,
and in waves we grow
This same water,
joined as we are, like the view of the moon,
breath of air sight of star….
This same water which shapes the outlines of these states,
slowly constant change destroys and creates.
This same water,
with a thought I am home,
I can see a face through a voice on the phone…
This same water,
yet stronger ties through we bind,
when the worst comes to find us the best do we find…..
This same water against us cannot win,
when it comes to end, we again begin…
I think of my father and mother every day,
and so much flashes over me in so many ways
I was blessed with love,
I was blessed with freedom,
I was blessed with support, and the power of duty and honor,
and those things which form that,
in the depths of my soul
I ventured out from the shores of my town,
to find the world beyond disillusioned often by the reality of the world,
and the way things are ready to fight
to make the ideal the reality…..
It’s hard to reconcile what is with what should be
in my inexperience of youth I allowed anger to get the best of me
I made mistakes,
went against even my own conscience
unable to accept injustice,
against those who wronged me, taking vengeance,
but vengeance is not justice,
and sometimes answers just don’t come easy
and there is a personal sadness when self reflection clearly sees
the path that could have been
But when those values and morals find their second wind
we come out on the other side
and with new resolve, if lucky,
learn how to put into practice
something so simple and basic....**

“Pecans”

It is winter here, near the mouth of the St. John's River,
starting between Halloween and before Thanksgiving,
when only a few trees leaves fall, no longer living.
Pecans begin to drop, and falling to stop on the ground with a sound,
of a thud, or a pop, if they hit something hard.

Trees discard leaves, except Live Oak, Mistletoe, and Pine....
It is not nearly as brown and gray, I would say,
as more northern latitudes of my youth...
Cold only comes in snaps, and I do miss the change of seasons.
When the leaves turn colors here it does not last as long,
and it is not as bright or vibrant, as temperate regions.
Not so much a winter thing, but an in between of Autumn and Spring....
As Christmas approaches even more nuts fall,
a squirrels' delight, and paradise.....

I gather up the bounty of these oval capsules,
camouflaged brownish tan with stripes of black,
peeling the meat within from cracked shells,
washing away brown frass from the two channels
found on either side of the each half of the kernel.
I cannot resist the temptation, and bite into a half,
moist yet firm and almost crunchy,
and examine the seed, dark brown skin with such light fruit inside.
Relative to the walnut, yet so much sweeter,
I cannot wait to add brown sugar to make a pie.

It is tedious work to shell pecans, but the reward so worth the effort.
A unique flavor, made more unique by adding butter and vanilla....
.... ahhh, Butter Pecan...
I can't think of anyone who doesn’t like pecan pie,
or butter pecan ice cream.

Pecan harvest feels slightly more like Thanksgiving than Christmas,
but it does mark the end of one season,
and the promise of another yet to come

"The Dutch Country"

**There is no marked gateway to an idyllic past,
but there are places where the past comes alive,
where time slows down,
and the trappings of the modern world are excluded and set aside.**

**When I was young my parents took me to the Pennsylvania Dutch
Country.
Not just to visit, but spending the summer camping in the Amish
countryside.
Days fishing in a pond, fond of running through fields of corn and beans,
On moonlit nights would sing songs on a horse drawn hayride.**

**Far from city lights, stars seemed to fill the skies.
Fireflies above dark fields dancing for my eyes.
The steady drum of machinery so prevalent in suburbia,
now silent, as simplicity slows the clocks of this Utopia.**

**Life took on a peaceful rhythm of day dark and light
Sunrise felt of rested energy, sunset of exhausted relaxation,
both being marked with purples, yellows, oranges, and reds.
The full moon would make fields of crops glisten like a sea at night.**

**I remember eating in Smorgasbord style, churning ice cream by hand,
riding in a horse drawn carriage, and making hay.
Riding on the Strasbourg Railroad, with trips to Hershey Park, and
Gettysburg.
A beauty in the simplicity of Amish life
which made me want to forever stay.**

**There were covered bridges, dried corn and apples, cider, and shoo fly pie.
The subtraction of distractions seemed to enrich life,
as more was lost there was more to gain.
I realized that we rely too much upon technology,
and that we serve it as slaves.
I realized the folly of our modern philosophy,
and that it lead to a spiritual grave.
I realized that honesty in lifestyle equated to honesty in life,
and that this was not common in the world from which I came.**

**We afford ourselves no time to think or reflect,
and not enough time for each other.
I was accepted at face value, and could safely wear my heart on my sleeve,
knowing each face as sister or brother.
Knowing there were no judgments being passed upon me except my own,
I know that the part of me I leave forever stays in my heart, like a home.**

"Parasitic Man and Earth"

Oh, Earth, is it your legacy to become so defiled?
It is we who let it get this way....
poisoned and polluted by corporations,
enabled by the power of purchased political consent of so many nations,
and supported by greed of need of comfort and convenience....

On, Man, rampant runs our thirst for toxic soup, the fuels of our self-destruction,
which we spoon feed our children until cancers manifest...
We ask self-delusively, "why me"?
We refuse to admit our own culpability,
as invasive species devastate ecosystems, and others face extinction.

Oh, Earth, your waters we have contaminated,
myriad trace toxins and heavy metals in living tissue,
carbon, methane, sulfur, and benzene...
filling our eyes and lungs, as rain becomes acidic,
and coral reefs and virgin forest vanish from the scene.
It is just so pathetic.

Oh, Man, how can anyone speak with criticism of those who would defend
against this assault upon this sacred process of life's cyclic journey,
as we trace our path through the Milky Way.....
We drift in swirling circles, in a galactic sea of 200 billion stars,
In a galactic community of two billion galaxies.....
for the last 14 billion years.
What makes us so special that we assume we can so disrespect,
the galactic womb of humanity, earth?
Against our own best interest's we wage war,
and the only way to win this battle is to stop it.

Oh, Earth, if I have assaulted you, may I now ask forgiveness?
Oh, Earth, if I have waged war may I now sue for peace and surrender?
Oh, Earth, may I be allowed to make amends for my senselessness,
and offer my soul, and all my strength render?
How can I be well if you are not?
Oh., Man, how can we stand being that which we all should not?
Do you not have self-awareness and conscience?
Will you exercise your ability to change?
Oh, Earth, forgive us.

“Veins of the Body of a Nation”

**Rails and trails,
roads and highways,
canals and rivers,
oceanic airways,
veins of the body of a nation.....**

**vehicular and mechanized blood cells,
flowing with movements like living flesh....
caught in a web of a sickening mesh....**

**Fuel and nutrients delivered in trucks and containers,
waste removed by dumpsters to landfill retainers,
water and sewers, and an electrical grid,
phones and the net, everywhere that we live.....**

**Observed in fast motion it all seems so alive,
spreading like a virus as nature slowly dies....
We consume and consume until everything's gone,
to be non-renewable is just simply wrong....**

**A parasite or cancer, I simply can't tell,
mankind's abuses in the body of a nation,
consuming and growing until our damnation.**

**But we have an option to choose not to be,
the kind of an organism that would kill water, sky, and sea,
and honor the earth and live symbiotic,
and choose life over death, and stop being psychotic.**

"Train Into The City"

Train into the city, destination, the night
Train on tracks of pity, passengers in flight,
train moves to with rhythm, tracks provide the beat
A steel snake that's living,
and all the dead cargo, just sit in their seats

Where will this ticket take me?
Mr. Conductor, please don't you fake me
Where is the last stop?
Tell me!
Tell me!
I gotta get off this train

Passengers on a time machine,
on schedule to the next stop
Perspectives changing with the scenes,
I'll always remember, what they forgot

Life is like a train, don't ya know,
keeps rolling on down the tracks.
And though return trips you can take, my dear,
you can never really ever,
no never go back

Where will this ticket take me?
Mr. Conductor, please don't you fake me.
Where is the last stop?
Tell me!
Tell me!
I gotta get off this train

"Working In The Heat Of The Day"

Heat of the day, money made by sweat
I'd pray for rain, but I'm already wet
Heat of the night, and I can't even sleep
I'm burning with promises made I must keep

It goes on and on and on,
and it takes way too long
to reach simple goals,
to sing a victory song
It goes on and on and on,
but I guess it's all okay
Somehow I feel whole
in the heat of the day

Hard work and respite,
famine and feast and inbetween
I could say the same for desolate cold,
these are just the things I've seen
And working in a heat wave,
like a fast track to a grave
Life so good can get so mean,
pennies earned with so few saved

And it goes on and on and on,
in the furnace is the working man
to forge out a better life
for wife, for kids, he must stand
and it goes on and on and on
and somehow it'll all be okay
and it always seems to long
working in the heat of the day

"In Midnight Stillness"

Silence in the night,
am I am accompanied by only my thoughts and emotions.
Thoughts and memories reflected by dim light,
yet I can see them more clearly in this solitude.

Finding acceptance with what is,
and letting go of what could have been,
gives me freedom to make better choices
and the will to meet a new day, and the day to begin.

We rush and hurry all too often,
and race our way to an urn or coffin.
I need time to digest the thoughts and emotions and events of my day,
and reflecting back in midnight stillness shouldn't be the only way.

The pace of life often shows how easily good efforts we waste,
in this endless race which feeds our strife we create ourselves in haste.
To take the time to adjust our course is all that I desire.
To make decisions in line with reason is a must if we are to aspire,
to be just a little more human, and act just a little more sane,
as we rush in constant madness, losing what we might never regain.

This is what I propound;
that each heart needs a refuge, to find the peaceful light,
and not a state of lack of sound is the silence in the deep of night.
The stillness is a frame of mind,
a place to go to see,
The path ahead and the path behind,
and who the heart will be.

Finding acceptance with what is,
and letting go of what could have been,
gives me freedom to make better choices
to meet a new day, and the day to begin.

"Random Words"

Random words just cast together,
and they've got the nerve to call it "poetry".
Paint just splattered on a canvas,
is it from an artist, or a child of three,
I really can't tell.

Have we really become so vain,
we now accept paying cash for trash,
what a shame.
And the things that made me glad, now make me sad,
and melancholy,
but that's just part of the game.

The name of the game is insanity,
and all humanity plays.
This time we find we call out rat race days.
And selfish souls with no self-control,
hold only one goal,
some kind of escape.
But there aren't really any that work,
Yeah, I guess we create our own fate.

And the random words jumbled loosely
profusely flow from warped minds.

And we, who understand the difference,
without resistance.....................

.......................resign.

“So Few See It Coming”

The rise and fall of civilizations,
cultural creations,
states and nations,
like tides,
rising and falling in cyclic motion,
shifted and changed by external forces,
beyond any measure of control......

Egyptian, Ottoman, Byzantine, Roman,
British, Spanish, Viking, Mayan......
Kingdoms and dynasties, rise and fall to dust;
concrete to crumble, steel to rust.

Each incarnation built with remnants of the past,
with one revelation, none forever will last.

Hubris and pride, and blindly we abide,
following a well worn path.
Growth and expansion until resources subside,
and then comes over-extension's wrath.

Yet blindly we ignore our date with impending doom,
and ridicule and abhor those who remind us, “soon”.
We continue to allow the wealthy to take advantage of the weak and poor,
and call them moral “traitors”, and to reason shut the door.

So few see it coming, and are ready for the brewing storm,
protecting knowledge with civility, as humanity again is torn,
The tools to build a better world are herenow in our grasp,
so seldom are they used before our empire breathes one last gasp.

Like a phoenix or a seed of renaissance a new society of man will arise,
but the cycle simply starts again in anthropology’s reprise.

“Watching Negative Utopias”

On the Beach, we’re melting away,
Great God, we’re all through,
Am I "I Robot", too?
Colossus, Metropolis,
Controls what I say and do
Orwell says it’s 84
And I can’t take it any more
There’s a Brave New World,
Waiting for me and you.
Feels like 451 in here,
Even Klattu ran in fear
911 on 9-11, all this oil just for fun
And all these nuts each have a gun
Watch all this blood just run and run…
Away......
I just want to run away

Dear God, can’t you hear the pleas
Of the innocent who drop down to their knees,
And take a bullet in the head,
They never listened to what you said…..
Hitler and The Jews,
And history now repeats
Jews do unto whom the choose,
And Palestine lies in ruins at our feet
And Muslims murder in God's name
As we arm both sides of this stupid game
And Hindus die in Pakistan
And Africa is burning land
North Korea kills another man
Just because he wants to stand
And drugs from Latin lands below
All these things just have to go
And Bush and Rush scream from the right,
What’s left in darkness is the light
Failing schools while jobs export
We follow fools of that sort
Just build more jails everywhere
And spit more carbon in the air
We’ve got our cable so just don’t care…
If there’s solutions just tell me where

("Watching Negative Utopias" continued)

**And I'll go……
To solve or escape,
I swear I'll go
To end greed, hate and rape, and know
The world just for once the way,
You would have hoped it'd be by now
I'd make it real, I don't know how….
It all ever got to be
A place when only few are free
And God in silence waits above,
For man to learn the gift of Love**

**On the Beach, we're melting away,
Great God, we're all through,
Am I "I Robot", too?
Colossus, Metropolis,
Controls what I say and do
Orwell says it's '84
And I can't take it any more
There's a Brave New World,
No soma kills the pain
Face it all day after day,
And never ever walk away
Still I want to run away**

**Dear God, can't you hear the pleas
Of the innocent who drop down to their knees,
And fight for humanity
One day when we all stand hand in hand
And plowshares are forged in every land
And gone are greed and insanity
And you and I can truly be,
Standing on the beach, as free
This is the day I live to see….
'Til then God sits in silence from above
Waits for us to find one love**

"Military Industrial Complex"

**How much soil has been soaked in blood.....
spoiled by the turbulence of war, like clean waters choked with mud....?
How many homes and villages have been razed to the ground....
ruins screaming or murder, rape, and pillage, now silent without a sound?**

**How many millions have died in genocide or war, from famine or disease?
What God do we serve and what God do we please?
Ignorance, greed and inequality creating fear, hate, jealousy, and rage.
If the Earth is a book and man just a chapter, please turn this page.**

**Reason remains so elusive....
and I just don't understand............
why the good remain silent, either paralyzed, or refusing to act....
....while the innocent and children suffer or die, from unavenged
attacks.....
and so few demand....................
strange the release of change and peace
I do not advocate violence, unless to defend those who are the most
vulnerable.....
....I hate the deeds of those whom I forgive with mixed emotions.
I pity those who simply cannot understand.... how to take a positive
stand.**

**How much profit will these corporations acquire,
before we stop consuming all these weapons we detest?
Their means justify their ends, it is wealth they desire,
they care for themselves, but never about the rest.**

**Military Industrial Complex crafts another gun,
and eventually every weapon made will one day wind up getting used.
When we export war we import death,
but this is the path chosen by those we choose.**

**Reason remains so elusive....
and I just don't understand............
why the good refuse to act, either paralyzed, or silent........while the
innocent and children suffer or die, from unavenged attacks...
so many, so violent....................
strange the release of change and peace
How those responsible culpable and defend those who are the most
vulnerable.....
....Hate the deeds of the spiritually small such as these
and forgive despite mixed emotions.
Teach those who simply cannot understand....
this is how to take a positive stand.**

"Plutocratic Dystopia"

IMF and the Fed, World Bank, and Wall Street,
board rooms and closed sessions, secret meetings at a retreat,
all the plutocrats, corporate fascists, dictators, and elites,
all striving for control, universal and complete.

They manipulate resources, currency, conflict, and war,
and sit back and laugh as the profits roll in.
Bull or Bear market, they still make their score,
and the 99 below just never win...

They own the minerals and oil, water and soil,
and do not care how the rest of us toil.
They make consumer goods, the guns and the cars,
they make the pharmaceuticals and alcohol we drink in bars.

They own the media and tell lies, and most conservatives comply.
They sell God and self-righteousness while committing genocide.
They tax the middle and poor, more and yet more,
to give cuts to affluent and corporate whores.

They kill what they touch and hurt what they can't,
then tell us they're moral in political rants.
And divide us to conquer, and in the end we all lose,
'til civility crumbles, another path we choose.

So with your wealth of education boycott their lies,
and find a new pathway before our civilization dies.

"Flag of a Better World"

I don't think any kind of master plan of world domination actually exists,
at least not in any form viable enough to succeed.
I do believe there are those who seek to dominate and profit from others,
and from their acts see they do not care who may cry, or who may bleed.

I believe that we are born with the capacity and desire to love
and be loved;
but I know that there are some
who reject their own conscience and humanity.
To think that in some ways we have become so advanced,
come so far,
yet in fear, jealousy, envy, or ignorance, resort to insanity.

The myriad means of self-destruction arise in successive waves,
and still some stand against the darkness defiantly.
Truth and compassion, the weapons of the warriors for peace and justice,
attacking the dark forces with gentle strength so silently,
as they absorb abuses delved out so violently,
these injuries that could break weaker spirits,
they bend to pliantly,
and mold themselves to fit into and build a better world,
and end ravages of greed, hate, and injustice, and inequity,
a new nation of man, a new flag of humanity unfurled.

The Flag of a Better World flies in my heart.
The idea is simple, that if we eliminate what motives one to abuse another,
that the abuse may also vanish.
If we view each other as neighbor, cousin,
sister and brother,
that much of the fear, jealousy, envy, or ignorance we may finally banish.
So I stand as just another warrior fighting for peace and justice,
that the task of building a better world
is something we may finally accomplish.

"Apartheid"

See the mothers cry as the tanks roll by,
I pray for the day that apartheid dies.
See the children play as the guns blow them away,
I pray for the day that apartheid dies....

Why must we live in a world of inequity,
where corporate fascists profit without morality,
where global powers turn blind eyes to depravity,
and human hearts in silence share complicity,
for the crimes of those whose inequities
run limitless unchecked.
And I elect
to use my power to stand with affinity,
with peace warriors I share unanimity.

See the drones in the sky as the innocent die,
I pray for the day that apartheid dies.
See the wall and the guard who makes life so hard,
I pray for the day that apartheid dies.
See the man with the bomb, and then he is gone,
I pray for the day that apartheid dies.
See the genocide, do you feel something human inside?
We should pray for the day that apartheid dies...

Why must we live in a world of injustice,
where what matters most to so many is their avarice,
where halfhearted overtures are just artifice,
and we patiently wait unsure of man's caprice,
for one step forward and to accomplish
one singular goal
And I elect
to use my power to stand with compassion
with peace warriors I choose to fight the oppression

See the flags they raise, blood soaked yet they are praised,
I pray for the day that apartheid dies.
God can't be on both sides yet in His name so many die,
I pray for the day that apartheid dies
See foundations shake as conscious choices we make,
Please pray for the day that apartheid dies.
I can't be silent or walk away and there's something I must say,
I live for the day that apartheid dies

“Multicolor Humanity”

Yellow, red, tan, brown, black, and white......
and skin a factor used to create divisions,
this I know, but cannot understand.
The multicolor patchwork of humanity,
blood below flowing either red or blue,
yet bigotry remains a continuing legacy of man.
This inescapable fact is sadly so true.

Vibrant colors of culture, light the far end of a prism,
light comprised of bandwidths some would exclude,
but doing so would make light incomplete and skewed,
and something would be lost.

Variety should be embraced, this multicolored humanity,
with realization that we are all essentially the same....
Yet we use language and lifestyle, religion and creed, politics and habits,
all to place barriers between each other like it was a game.
We should be looking for pathways to love each other in friendship,
rather than oppose each other and create conflict without reason.

My heart sees the beautiful picture painted by a multicolored humanity,
and my soul cries out for an end to divisions.
I just do not understand our self-imposed insanity.

Vibrant colors of culture, light the far end of a prism,
light comprised of bandwidths none should exclude,
Doing so would make light complete, ourselves renewed,
and nothing would be lost.

“Uncivilized Civilization”

**Civilization of the uncivilized, with materialism so adored,
where is your civility?
As the debates of the human animal consume resources beyond sustainability,
warnings of rational minds which foresee impending doom remain grossly ignored.
Where is the pathway to peace and prosperity so many desire?
Where is the promise of the human heart's fire?**

**Oil and water, education and technology, climate change and extinction,
and no decisive actions of distinction.**

**So many civilizations which have come before have fallen,
with so many advancements lost in the wake of their destruction.
How is it man can place so much suffering
and abuse upon their fellow man?
This I can know, but could never understand.**

**Are we so trapped by our habits that we ignore--
the knock upon our door?
And those who light the way to a better day stay,
working to awaken sleepers.
So few rise like the sun to shine with the power of truth and reason.
So many in darkness pledge allegiance to love, but are guilty of treason.**

**We must care for each other and care for our earth,
knowing that we are all connected, and share our destiny or fate.
But the darkness is coming and it cannot be averted.
The best we can do is mitigate growing adversity,
and aspire to the higher ideals which can make us great,
leaving no one deserving deserted.**

**Those who fear the future can choose to meet it with courage.
The decision to act upon the dictates of true conscience create rage.
It is clear that faith, hope, and love can conquer the scourge,
of the dark hearts so selfish and cold......
and so the future will unfold.....
and the story of man will start a new page......**

Equity, peace, compassion and human dignity, when will it come to pass?

**Civilization of the uncivilized, with materialism so adored,
where is your civility?**

"Stop!"

Hey, there, little one,
when it seems your world's come undone,
you play all day yet nothings fun,
feels like you're always under the gun

So you look up towards the sky,
with a million questions why,
and no one see the tear in your eye,
for all the futures you know will die

Stop! the world spinning for just a moment
Stop the war, stop the hate, the postponement...
Stop! and remember that under earth sun,
from love comes birth, and we all are one

Hey there very old one, with all the things you've seen and done,
you wonder why thing's have come so undone, and all you want do is run

So you teach all that you've learned,
to shut minds and doors where lands burned
words of wisdom ignored and spurned,
while peace is still the thing most yearned

Stop! in your tracks and stand demanding,
for a world of love understanding
Stop! and give humanity just one more chance,
in joy and in step with life's dance

Hey there, little one, listen close, a secret comes,
the old one there will show you a path, and if you listen some good may pass

Then, when the walls fall that divide us,
and we release the beauty inside us
eyes, will see love in thy neighbor,
and pain will pass like a birth's labor

Stop! The world spinning for just a moment,
Stop the war, stop the hate, no postponement
Go! With integrity towards a new day
we must stop and find a new way......
Stop!

"Elusive Understanding"

An electro-chemical process......
this metamorphosis of matter and energy,
and the evolution of its' form,
this thing which we call life......
an endless process of change
flowing through the constant now,
in motion rearrange.
Born
of particle waves that resonate in frequencies of light,
radio waves,
and sound,
in sight.
The repulsions,
the attractions,
and the static neutrality,
coalescing in a myriad of matrixes,
a dance of reactions,
birth,
life,
and mortality, simply interactions.
We attach novice understanding with words like
dimension,
micro,
macro,
and quanta we cannot quantify.
Yet we can only make educated guesses as to how it all formed,
and have no idea of of what was,
will be,
or came before......
And so we look within and without,
observe,
investigate,
deduce,
conclude,
delude,
and look again once more.
a thirst to assign reasons why,
instead of accepting,
what simply is.
Life to live and die.

"Trappings of the Heart or Prior Commitments"

**Truth has a way of catching up in night's solitude;
without having to sneak, it softly creeps in.
Realities of life are brought into focus,
and "what ifs" whisper idyllic pictures of what could of,
should of.....
and I am blinded by the sound of my own heart.
Myself I pound, I tear apart.....
and I curse the blessing of commitments of love.**

**These made commitments I must by abide,
but some of the reasons I made them have died,
much like martyrs sacrificed to the trappings of the heart.
I am resolved to at least a few final attempts,
to see the reaping of seeds sown,
the fruition of possibilities known;
but I can no longer suffer like the victim of succubi.
"Prior commitments" are not enough a reason
to allow the beauty left inside to die.**

**I can no longer be a wellspring of hope,
my aquifer is exhausted, and must be replenished....
and there is dryness in the sky I share,
with my contractual obligations......
It is sad to see that which I have invested of myself wither,
but maybe commitments and their trappings are subject to seasons...
and despite a harvest winter comes.
I shall glean the fields for remnants of past bounty,
sustenance for the journey through solstice to next spring...
… when I may plant again,
a more insightful farmer.**

**Melancholy mixture of warm reflection and regret,
and will it not accept being any longer hushed or silenced.
Somber in the stillness of night, as truth an audience demands,
and I realize with sad smile that these thoughts are most clear at night,
and that what comes tomorrow is morning light,
and what one inner voice refuses and denies,
another understands.**

"She Doubts Herself"

**She doubts herself, through flowing tears and medications;
blames herself for abuses made by others,
those who say they love or care.....
.... but when needed are never there.**

**Why is she so ill equipped to deal with this world?
I think she, a tender heart, is just too kind,
or maybe expects too much.
She would benefit from growing just a little bit cynical,
and more self-defensive.**

**She must love and respect herself,
this before she can ever expect others to,
and that is the threshold she must cross.
She knows these things,
but maybe doesn't have the faith in them,
or herself,
enough to find that to gain she must choose loss......**

**Sometimes to move ahead we need to make a 180,
then with one step just start again,
her forward motion so shaky,
and she just wants the touch of the hand of a friend,
because she doubts herself.**

**I tell her to accept it all for what it is,
there is no expectation of reason, sanity, honesty or kindness,
and not to expect others to live up to standards they just don't possess,
To meet the world eyes open, and not chosen blindness.....**

**Grow a spine, words easily said,
but most things are more easily said than done...
It'll be fine,
ease your heart, rest your head,
you're not there yet, but it will come....
it is okay, I tell her, to doubt herself,
as long as she fights a little more than she surrenders,
and remember that she's never alone,
that as long as I breathe she has a defender...**

"5 a.m."

It's 5 am, the world awakes,
I think of you again, and my body shakes...
and as I give up, in submission to this fate,
again and again and again,
no matter how long it takes....

In a cup of coffee, I see my reflection,
a tear in silence on my cheek my detection
and as I give out, in submission to this fate,
again and again and again,
no matter how long my heart breaks.....

I'm reaching out to you, to love you like none before, can't you see this love true?
I'm reaching into your soul, to break through all locked doors,
until we both lose control.
I'm reaching out for your heart, can't you feel my love as it moves?

As the sun breaks the night, and I greet a new day,
I remember why I fight for love to come then stay
And as I give up, in submission to this fate
again and again I wait
no matter how long it takes

I shut my eyes, yet can't escape your face,
this tear I realize reminds me of the empty spacc
and as I resolve, to pick up and carry on,
again and again and again,
no matter how long.....it takes

I'm reaching out to you, to love you like none before,
can't you see this love is true?
I'm reaching into your soul, 'til we're complete as love makes us whole,
what else can I do?
I reaching out for your heart, can't you feel my spirit move?

It's 5 0 1, and the world awakes...
I think of you again.......

"Come Hither Here"

Come hither here me Bonnie Lass, and let me feel your hand...
The winds are hard, and I am scarred, by the wrongs I'd to withstand...
But stand I do, and even now,
with faith and love untold,
and if I could, you know I would, you hand I'd take and hold

Love, love, is all we lack,
and all we truly need...
To stand so true, and make it through,
to the place we want to be...
Love, love, is we all must have,
it's the treasure of the soul,
and we find it in each others' eyes, when we live, let life unfold...

Come hither here, me Bonnie Lass, come take now my hand,
and we'll both stand firm, we'll live and learn, and the hard winds we'll withstand...
And stand we will, from now until, we both grow old and die,
and in the ground, we'll hear this sound,
as we lay there side by side....

Love, love, is all they knew,
and all they ever had...
and hand in hand, their children stand,
against hard winds, not sad..
The lessons learned from a Bonnie Lass,
and her light and love, her man
served them well, and this truth I tell...
this you must understand....

Love, love, is all we need,
it's the best thing we can give...
and by good heart, and in good deed,
that legacy will live...
Love, love, is we have,
it's the treasure of the soul
So find your love, and stand your ground,
Come hither, here, and hold
Come hither, here, and hold
To the love that's in your soul
To the love that's in your soul

"Sunrise"

**The sunrise was so beautiful,
as it was coming up over the trees
My mind was set on being free,
it was playing with the birds and the bees...
I decided to talk a walk that morning,
to see what I could see
my heart is my compass and my shoes are my home,
taking life, naturally**

**Sunrise...........
as the world cycles round once again
Sunrise............
as we're hurled there's a sound that never ends
Sunrise..............
You can surf gravity and never fall
Sunrise...............
and Eternity doesn't take too long at all
Sunrise.... Sunrise..... I'll answer the call**

**The Sunrise was so beautiful,
as it was coming up over the sea
waves rhythm reprise, I realize,
in the end I'm just who I'm supposed to be
I decided to stop and rest a while,
smile at all I've seen
The good and the bad, the happy and sad
taking life, naturally**

**Sunrise.............
Can say volumes without a word
Sunrise.............
The best silence ever heard
Sunrise.............
The world spins around once again
Sunrise..............
Single step to a dance that don't end
Sunrise.... Sunrise.....
my beautiful friend**

"You & I"

You and I, will never find the deepest parts,
until, we try,
to to touch the sky, to reach the shores,
to stand, side by side,
live and love, like in days gone by

You, and I, must walk the path,
to reach the end,
to see, eye to eye,
to build this love and make it last,
to stand side by side,
just like love was in days gone by

When we lived, when we touched,
when we gave, no matter how hard or how much,
when we laughed, when we cried,
when we stood even when we died
when we held, held on strong,
even though if felt as if it all took too long,
So we reach, reach inside,
just to try
to find the way back to a world gone by.....

You and I, join as one
just like that day, we came, to say,
standing side by side, we made, a vow, to stay,
the way we are right now, inside,
just like love was in days gone by
When we knew, what we know,
and were true, true enough to show
show the love , deep inside, that we share,
and never fear or hide,
now I pledge, as do you, to face this life,
and see everything through,
til we reach, the very end,
and our days go by for a message to send,
to the ones, who follow, and
will make days gone by never end

"Patiently"

I can taste you in my mind, intelligent and sublime....
I have, waiting, so long for this thing to find

I am patient, with resolve....
waiting, for this thing between- to evolve

Should we attempt to discover, are you willing,
brave enough to glimpse
past
this veil that shrouds what could be?

Seeming still, my mind races, like my heart which pounds
anticipation of the flavors
of what I hope- may yet become

You see the surface, like ripples upon the water
the shimmer of reflected sky,
and as deep as the atmosphere is high

I want to know your deepest thoughts, dreams, desires...
your fires
of epiphany

Take a moment, and in silence gaze,
with somber reflection,
and see why my eyes say to your heart

you will not hear those unspoken words in others
you will not see your heart waiting for you in them
waiting
patiently

for you to see
that part of yourself
in me

“Gently”

Very, gently, I took your hand,
at the beach, on the sand.

Very, softly, you took my heart,
knew the play, played your part.

And we danced in magical circles,
with the waves lapping over our feet.
In a sky of orange and purple,
we surrendered without defeat.
Then we looked into the horizon,
it seemed as endless as our love.

So com-pletely, we join as one,
under the stars, under the sun.

Very, truly, I make this vow,
to live for love, forever and now.

And we reached the best in each other,
by sharing the best of ourselves.
Companions, friends, and lovers,
ready for the stories this life shared tells.
Then we saw deep into the horizon,
it was as endless as our love.

Very, gently, I took your hand.

"Gravity"

The pull of gravity,
the attraction that one body of mass has upon another.......
Our mass, our being, our essence,
is drawn down to the earth's core.

So, this attraction keeps us grounded,
without which we would lack the ability to know how to stand upright.
Our moon, and even our sun, pulls upon us,
like it pulls water to creates tides...
away from our grounding sphere,
so we are compelled to look beyond our world.

Like love, one drawn to the other,
yet symbolizing so much more,
without heavy one cannot know light,
like the difference between day and night,
This sensation, these thoughts from deep inside.........

Minute as it may be, we generate our own individual magnetic fields,
maybe other kinds of fields as well.
On some level we must be aware of the connection we have to each other,
which is why we sense each other on mysterious and undefined levels.....

We are drawn together, connected, bound eternally joined.
Forms of energy acting with mimicry of gravity,
so that we look to define ourselves beyond our own self,
in the swirling mystery of the divine,
where we find parts of our own souls, within each other.

"Two Trillion"

Twilight Sky, after two trillion sunrises, two trillion sunsets..........
what stories the clouds could tell
if their memory wasn't washed away as rain.......

Twilight Dawn, marking the birth of a new day, the passing away-
-of night
Twilight Eve, reflection of thoughts and deeds in refractions of light

Sky above the Earth so eternal and vast,
and as upon this surface. when I face Sol in daylight,
Alas,
I am fooled into thinking clouds and soft blue mark where the sky ends,
and turns dark....
but at night, as where I stand faces away from my home sun,
the deep black of night and countless stars are my sky,
and it seems to go on forever, and ever
and I feel so small,
and yet part of something so amazingly large,
and endless,
and timeless.......

Sol, along with this my Earth, with me standing upon it,
and I,
outward seeing,
are but a twinkle of light in the night sky, of some distant being,
or at least may be, when Sol, Earth,
and I,
glisten through the fourth dimension,
reaching through this Milky Way, this Universe, through time and space...

And in the twilight sky I recognize a transition,
between limits and limitless...
between eternity and mortality....
between what never changes as it changes
and what is changing as it never changes....

Twilight Sky, after two trillion sunrises, two trillion sunsets..........
what stories the clouds could tell
if their memory wasn't washed away as rain.....

"Oh, Earth"

**Oh, Earth, is it your legacy to become so defiled?
It is we who let it get this way....
poisoned and polluted by corporations,
enabled by the power of purchased political consent of so many nations,
and supported by greed of need of comfort and convenience....**

**On, Man, rampant runs our thirst for toxic soup, the fuels of our self-destruction,
which we spoon feed our children until cancers manifest...
We ask self-delusively, "why me"?
We refuse to admit our own culpability,
as invasive species devastate ecosystems, and others face extinction.**

**Oh, Earth, your waters we have contaminated,
myriad trace toxins and heavy metals in living tissue,
carbon, methane, sulfur, and benzene...
filling our eyes and lungs, as rain becomes acidic,
and coral reefs and virgin forest vanish from the scene.
It is just so pathetic.**

**Oh, Man, how can anyone speak with criticism of those who would defend
against this assault upon this sacred process of life's cyclic journey,
as we trace our path through the Milky Way.....
We drift in swirling circles, in a galactic sea of 200 billion stars,
In a galactic community of two billion galaxies.....
for the last 14 billion years.
What makes us so special that we assume we can so disrespect,
the galactic womb of humanity, earth?
Against our own best interest's we wage war,
and the only way to win this battle is to stop it.**

**Oh, Earth, if I have assaulted you, may I now ask forgiveness?
Oh, Earth, if I have waged war may I now sue for peace and surrender?
Oh, Earth, may I be allowed to make amends for my senselessness,
and offer my soul, and all my strength render?
How can I be well if you are not?
Oh., Man, how can we stand being that which we all should not?
Do you not have self-awareness and conscience?
Will you exercise your ability to change?**

Oh, Earth, forgive us.

“Figure It Out”

**I could figure it all out, and everything understand.
I could accumulate knowledge, know the entire history of earth and man.
I could understand the secrets of physics and the scientific.
I could go as far as reading thoughts or become telekinetic and terrific.
I could glimpse foretell the future like a mystic or a profit.
I could evolve into a being compassionate as God.
Where would any of that get me in the end?
No joy of discovery, a sail without a wind.**

Too much of anything too good could wind up being bad.

**If I knew everything which came before,
would I be able to prevent others from opening
the mistakes of history's door?
If I knew all the secrets the sciences could explain,
what would be left to discover or learn or proclaim?
If I knew the thoughts of others what fun would conversation be,
with exciting bits of mysterious minds disclosed what new could I see?
If I could move things with my mind, what motivation is to move myself?
If I saw the future could I change it, or get others to change themselves?
If I knew the meaning of life, secrets of the Universe,
what would draw my interest?**

**With a chance at new discovery there is little sense of wonder,and none
would lift the mystery stone if they already knew what was there, under.
What tasteless food, what colorless sky, when all too much is known,
With omnipotent power discovery would die,
sad a king upon such a throne.
If a sentient all knowing God had such power,
He'd use His power to forget,
and allow freewill, chance, and destiny to disclose fate, glory, or regret.**

**I do not believe God or gods control too much,
it would be a pointless waste of time,
but this is the religious fanatic's crutch,
because they just don't have a spine.
Not what you say or what you pray, but deeds will win salvation,
judged mainly by our own conscience, hell or heaven our own creation....
I am happy that I know so much that I know I won't fully understand,
any reason for my own origin or existence,
I'm just an ape who chose to stand.
And I understand with such clarity, that God still has a voice,
Love is still worth risk and pain. Faith and goodness are a free will choice.
And so I choose to stand alone, and in vulnerability join with others,
Because I am strongest when I admit my weaknesses,
and at my best when I am one with my sisters and brothers.**

“Eternity”

Grasses blades bite the back of my neck,
a sky I am in,
a world I detect.

No sounds but nature, no soul but the Earth,
I have died as a mortal,
as a spirit have birth.

I look to the sky and I see my reflection,
To live as a Spirit of Love my election.

My Heart shines a mystery,
My Soul hears the sound,
as I drift towards eternity,
as I lie on the ground

"Dust"

Do I dare this showing?
I,
with self-awareness,
and a sense of knowing
I am,
I.

Looking outward and inward,
I am awkward, a coward,
maybe,
for forgetting
I am
but dust.

I,
a remnant of a star's death,
I,
both energy and matter,
two forms of the single "Essence",
a dissipating utterance beneath God's breath....

Logical conclusions illusions shatter,
these states of Mass/Energy with sentience coalescence,
and in the applied context of time,
I am
but dust.

www.ingramcontent.com/pod-product-compliance
Ingram Content Group UK Ltd.
Pitfield, Milton Keynes, MK11 3LW, UK
UKHW041837200726
13854UKWH00003BA/1180